SPANISH AMERICAN WAR OF 1898

HISTORY FOR KIDS

CAUSES, SURRENDER & TREATIES

TIMELINES OF HISTORY FOR KIDS
6TH GRADE SOCIAL STUDIES

On this book, we're going to talk about the history of the Spanish American War. So, let's get right to it!

The Spanish-American War began in 1898 and only lasted a period of about 6 weeks. It was later called "a splendid little war." The United States was victorious against Spain. As a result, Cuba became independent from Spain, and the United States gained new territories that once belonged to Spain.

SPANISH AMERICAN WAR

USA FLAGS AND UNITED STATES CAPITOL BUILDING

THE EMPIRES OF EUROPE

In the late 1800s, the European nations were very powerful and they were building their empires on both the continent of Asia and the continent of Africa. The United States was becoming increasingly powerful as well. Many citizens in the US, including governmental leaders, thought that the United States should continue to annex new territories too.

However, there was a lot of divided thinking about this because the United States had once been Britain's colony. The United States government and culture was built upon the fact that its citizens had broken away from their parent country in Europe. Growing a huge empire with colonies all over the world didn't seem like the right path for the United States, but there was no denying that the United States was on its way to becoming a world power.

HAWAII STATE CAPITOL BUILDING

Because of this history, at the beginning, it appeared that the United States wouldn't succumb to empire building. However, in the year 1893, there was an attempt to overthrow the government in Hawaii. At that time, Hawaii was not part of the United States.

US citizens who owned plantations there wanted to grab up the Hawaiian Islands for the US. At the beginning, the United States didn't support this effort. Then, in 1895, there was an uprising in Cuba and the part the United States played shaped the future history of North and South America.

AGRICULTURAL WORKERS ON A PLANTATION IN HAWAII

CUBAN FLAG

TROUBLE ERUPTS IN CUBA

Shortly after the unrest in Hawaii, there were more problems brewing in Cuba. The European country of Spain had been governing the island of Cuba for over three centuries. The citizens of Cuba wanted independence and they rose up against the Spanish.

The Spanish wanted to squelch this rebellion quickly. They had no intention of giving up Cuba. They forced many Cubans into camps. The conditions in the camps were deplorable and thousands of Cubans died from disease.

THE EPIC
More Bitterly
Than D-Da
LOSSES AM
ASMARA · TUESDAY 7th NOVEMBER 1944 ·
Eritrean
TIMES RUSSIA TO LOAN NEGOTIA
No. 1444
COPY IS FREE - MAKE SURE THAT
Eritrean Daily News
ENGLISH EDITION
PRICE: 10 C
* THE SUPPLEMENT OF THIS COPY IS FREE - MA
Eritrean Daily
ASMARA - SUNDAY 31st DECEMBER 1944 - No. 1,090
ENGLISH EDITION
RUNDSTEDT'S OFFENSIVE I.
Watches Gradual Disintegration
Of His Might
ALLIES STAND READY TO STRIKE FIERCE BLOWS
RUNDSTEDT'S OFFENSIVE IS FIZZLING OUT anti-climatically, cables Doon Camp-
bell, Reuters' special correspondent on the Western Front. Allied armies — a powerful new
potential offensive weapon — stand aggressively before Rundstedt's spent might ready to strike
pile-driving blows. The German commander, continues Campbell, is watching the gradual disinte-
gration of his 300,000 assault troops, his tanks, guns and planes — committed
yesterday.
He has lost the initiative of offensive, thousands of per
and stores of ammunition, transport and vital
man attack at Elsenborn, six mil
out positions, say
A Happy Ne
Year
THE EDITOR AND STAFF
THE 'ERITREAN DAILY NEW
THE PUBLIC INFORMATIC
OFFICER AND PERSONNEL O
THE BRITISH MINISTRY O
INFORMATION, ERITREA
WISH ALL OUR READERS AN
ADVERTISERS A HAPPY, AND
PROSPEROUS NEW YEAR
AS NEW YE

YELLOW JOURNALISM

The editors of American newspapers quickly pounced on this story and sensationalized it. Their goal was to get people interested and emotionally involved so they could sell a lot more newspapers.

Some of what they reported was true, but some of what they wrote was designed to ignite an emotional response and wasn't always based on fact. The process of using journalism that isn't based solely on facts and is designed to ignite emotions with sensational headlines is called "yellow journalism."

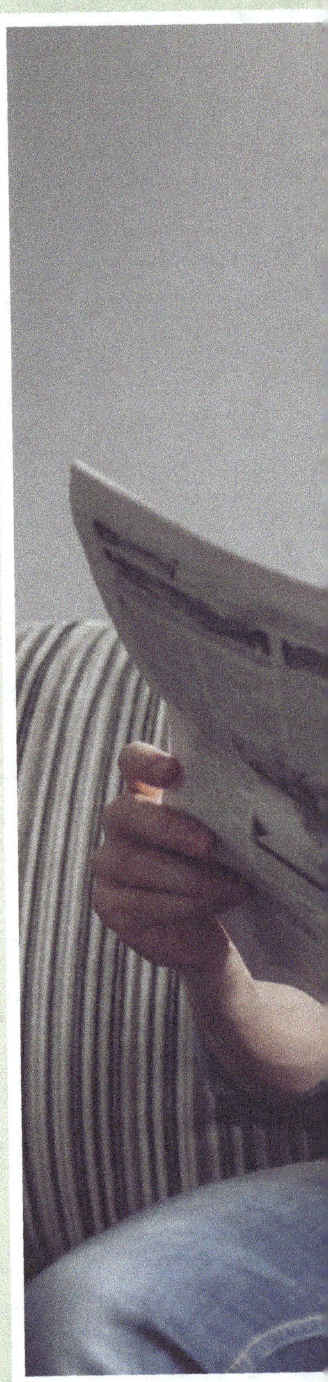

FATHER AND SON READING THE NEWSPAPER

REVOLUTIONARY WAR

The newspaper articles emphasized the similarities between the Cubans fighting for their independence and the Americans fighting in the Revolutionary War to be freed from Britain. The American public sided with the Cuban underdogs since they identified with their fight against Spain.

THE EXPLOSION OF THE USS MAINE

Because Cuba was so close to the United States in terms of geography, the US had many assets there. To protect their interests in Cuba, the US government sent a warship into the harbor located at the city of Havana.

FORT IN HAVANA, CUBA

THE DESTRUCTION OF THE BATTLESHIP
MAINE IN HAVANA HARBOR

The name of the ship was the USS Maine. After the ship had been docked there for only 9 days, it succumbed to an explosion and more than 200 Americans on board were killed. The Spanish said they had nothing to do with it. Later, it was confirmed that their statement was true, but many Americans believed that the Spaniards had sunk the ship on purpose.

Both countries tried to discuss what had happened, but the conflict just got worse. The United States Congress declared that a state of war existed between the two countries as of April 1898. Congress also approved the Teller Amendment. This Amendment stated that the United States would help the Cubans win their freedom, but that they would not annex Cuba as a US territory.

THE SPANISH-AMERICAN WAR BEGINS

The ships that the Spaniards had in the New World were in bad shape. They were no match for the new United States warships. The US captured the Philippines, which belonged to the Spanish. The citizens there also wanted freedom from the Spanish.

However, on the land, the battle wasn't as easy. The United States had put together a group of volunteer soldiers who weren't prepared for the harsh conditions of the tropical climate. Theodore Roosevelt, who was nicknamed "Teddy" and who would later become President, put together a cavalry division.

THEODORE ROOSEVELT

COLONEL ROOSEVELT AND HIS ROUGH RIDERS

They named themselves the "Rough Riders." Teddy and his cavalry forces were successful, which made him very popular with the American people. One of the reasons his forces were successful was because there were experienced African-American soldiers on his team.

Despite the hazards of the environment, the United States was victorious in six weeks. After the conflict, Cuba as well as the Philippines were under the control of the US. Then, the US became concerned that their interests in Hawaii were vulnerable. President William McKinley decided that the United States should take over Hawaii before Japan decided to annex it. Hawaii was taken over by the US in July of 1898.

WILLIAM MCKINLEY

JOHN HAY

Less than 400 Americans had died in the Spanish-American conflict and much had been gained. John Hay, who was the Secretary of State at that time, called the conflict "a splendid little war." However, what isn't often mentioned is that 5,000 additional Americans died from tropical diseases such as malaria.

THE TREATY OF PARIS

In the final months of 1898, representatives from Spain and the US had a meeting to discuss the final resolution. The Treaty of Paris listed the terms of the agreement:

- Spain freed Cuba
- Guam became a US territory
- Puerto Rico became a US territory
- The US paid $20 million to annex the Philippines as a US territory

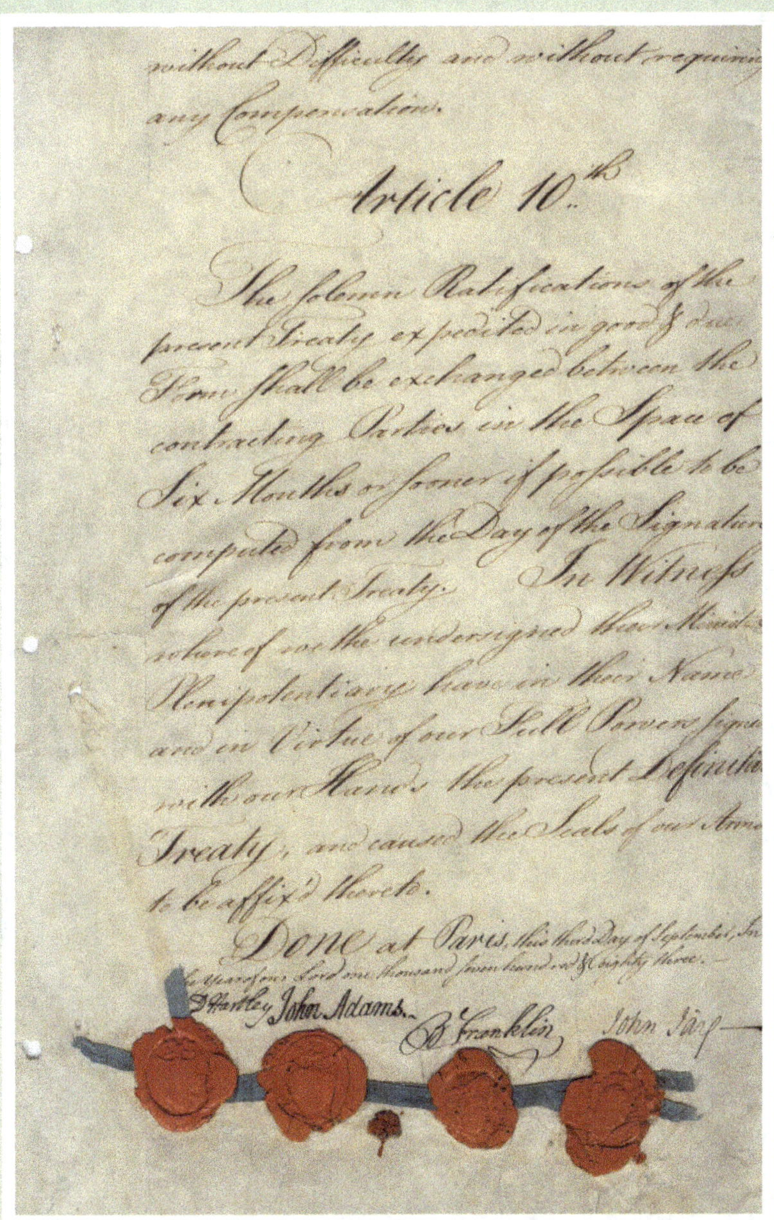

without Difficulty and without requiring any Compensation.

Article 10th.

The solemn Ratifications of the present Treaty expedited in good & due Form shall be exchanged between the contracting Parties in the Space of Six Months or sooner if possible to be computed from the Day of the Signature of the present Treaty. In Witness whereof we the undersigned their Ministers Plenipotentiary have in their Name and in Virtue of our Full Powers signed with our Hands the present Definitive Treaty, and caused the Seals of our Arms to be affixd thereto.

Done at Paris, this third Day of September In the Year of our Lord one thousand seven hundred & Eighty three.

D Hartley   John Adams   B Franklin   John Jay

SECOND PAGE OF TREATY OF PARIS

Although they were now supposedly free, citizens of Cuba and citizens of the Philippines weren't allowed to attend the negotiations. The United States now had territories that weren't states and had become like the countries in Europe with its own empire.

MAP OF THE PHILIPPINES

CONSEQUENCES FOR CUBA AND FOR THE PHILIPPINES

The US didn't take Cuba, but they had quite a bit of control over Cuba and this was detailed in the new constitution of that country. The Platt Amendment, allowed the US the right for intervention in diplomatic as well as economic and military channels. The Americans also had the right to rent Guantánamo Bay. The United States still has a military prison there today.

GUANTÁNAMO BAY

AMERICAN SOLDIERS IN THE PHILIPPINES
DURING THE SPANISH-AMERICAN WAR, CAVITE, MAY 3, 1898

The Filipinos had helped the United States get rid of the Spaniards in their country, the Philippines. They didn't get their freedom as they had expected. The United States government didn't believe that the Filipino people could rule themselves. When the Filipinos realized that the Americans had simply traded places with the Spanish, they began to rise up.

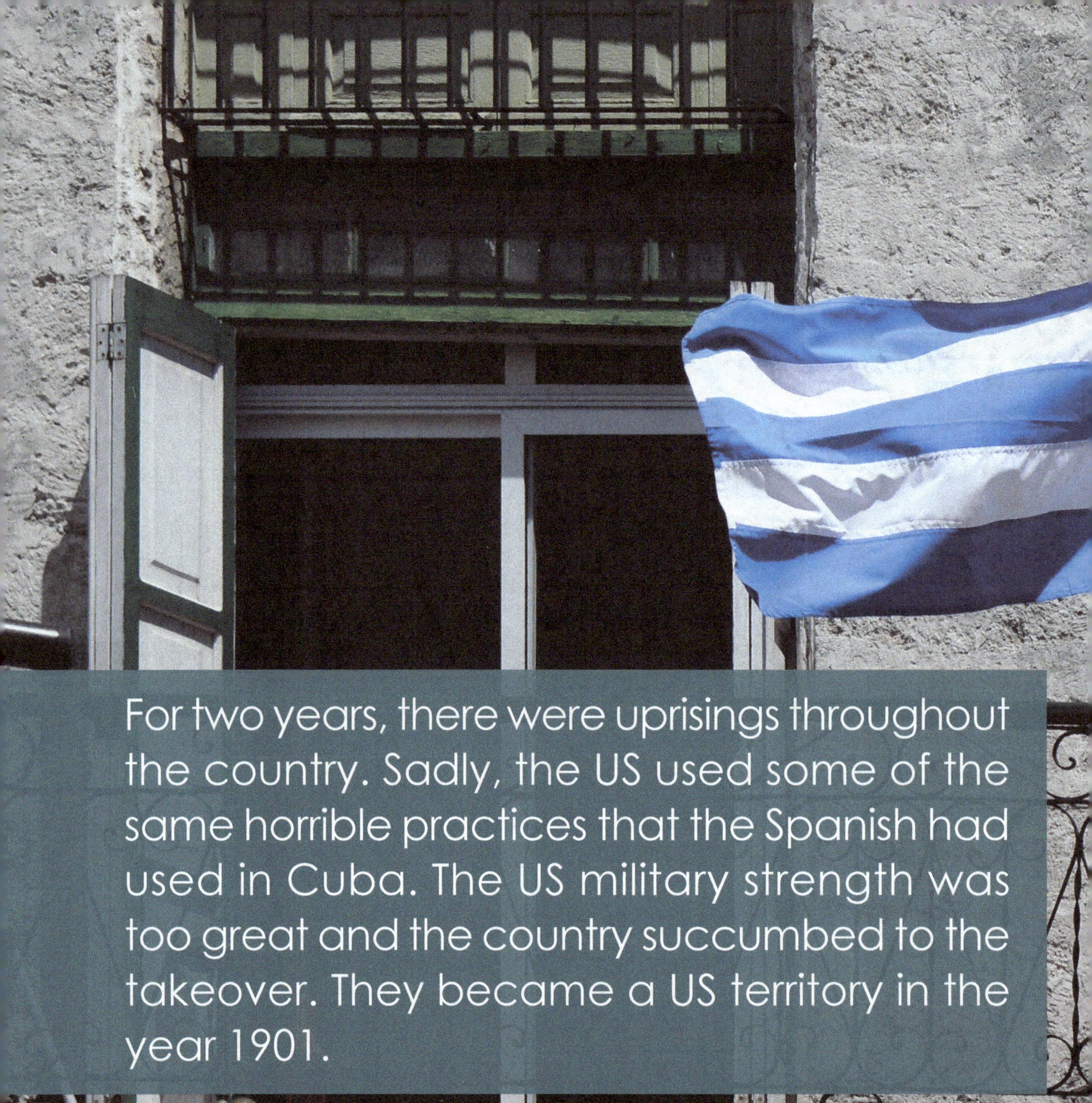

For two years, there were uprisings throughout the country. Sadly, the US used some of the same horrible practices that the Spanish had used in Cuba. The US military strength was too great and the country succumbed to the takeover. They became a US territory in the year 1901.

FILIPINO PRISONERS OF WAR

Prior to the Spanish-American War, the US had made the territories it gained into states. This was the first time that the US had gained territories without the ultimate goal of statehood. The Puerto Ricans eventually gained citizenship, but that Filipinos did not.

The United States had evolved from a nation that was isolated from world powers to an empire with its own territories. For better or for worse, it was now a global power.

U.S. FLEET IN THE BATTLE OF MANILA BAY

TIMELINE OF THE SPANISH-AMERICAN WAR

Here are some of the major events of the Spanish-American War:

April 1898—Congress states that the US is at war with Spain.

May 1898—The first battle takes place. Warships from the United States defeat the Spanish navy at Manila Bay. The Philippines has been taken by the US.

June 1898—US armies arrive on Cuban soil.

July 1898—The United States wins the battle at San Juan Heights on July 1st. On July 3rd, the US destroys the Spanish ships in Cuba's Santiago Bay. On July 17, the Spanish concede and the war is over.

August 1898—The United States and Spain sign a preliminary agreement to stop the war.

December 1898—The Treaty of Paris is approved. The United States has control of Cuba even though it is supposedly independent. Puerto Rico and the Philippines become US territories, so does Guam.

BATTLE OF SANTIAGO BAY

THE BATTLE OF LAS GUASIMAS

SUMMARY

The Spanish-American War was started because the Cubans wanted independence from Spain. Ignited by the rantings of yellow journalism, the American people wanted to assist the Cubans in their cause. Within 6 weeks, the United States was victorious against Spain. Cuba and the Philippines were now independent from Spain but had come under the control of the United States.

Awesome! Now that you've read about the history of the Spanish American War, you may want to read about the Mexican American War in the Baby Professor book, *Mexican American War 1846 - 1848 - Causes, Surrender and Treaties | Timelines of History for Kids | 6th Grade Social Studies.*

www.ingramcontent.com/pod-product-compliance
Lightning Source LLC
Chambersburg PA
CBHW060133120726
48003CB00009B/2876